THE
LITTLE
BOOK OF
PLANTING
TREES

MAX ADAMS is a critically acclaimed biographer and archaeologist and the author of eight books, including the best-selling *The King in the North* and *The Wisdom of Trees*. A teacher of woodland and tree histories, he manages an area of woodland in County Durham.

ALSO BY MAX ADAMS

Admiral Collingwood
The King in the North
In the Land of Giants
The Wisdom of Trees
Ælfred's Britain
Unquiet Women

THE
LITTLE
BOOK OF
PLANTING
TREES

MAX ADAMS

An Anima Book

This Anima book was first published in the UK
in 2019 by Head of Zeus Ltd
This Anima paperback edition first published in the UK
in 2020 by Head of Zeus Ltd

9 7 5 3 1 2 4 6 8

A catalogue record for this book is available
from the British Library.

ISBN (PB): 9781789545883

ISBN (E): 9781788546263

Typeset by Adrian McLaughlin
Chapter-opening linocuts by Sarah Price

Printed and bound in Great Britain by
CPI Group (UK) Ltd, Croydon CR0 4YY

Head of Zeus Ltd
5–8 Hardwick Street
London EC1R 4RG

WWW.HEADOFZEUS.COM

For Amanda, in memory of Julian Gaze

CONTENTS

INTRODUCTION

The Little Book of Planting Trees is a practical guide, intended to help and encourage those who have never planted a tree in their lives – yet. It is meant to inspire gardeners, school teachers and their pupils, those who have spotted a little patch of land in their neighbourhood where trees might do very well and the dreamers who want to create a new woodland where there was none before.

I am an archaeologist, concerned with understanding human relations with the landscape over the last few thousand years. But I have also been involved with planting, growing, felling and studying trees for more than a quarter of a century. They have taught me much about nature and about the history of our interactions with the natural world. After managing both mature and neglected woods, I now have my own young plantation of about 3 hectares (8 acres) close to the border between County Durham and Northumberland. Thistle Wood is endlessly fascinating. Watching trees – about 4,500 of them – grow from scratch on such a scale has been a revelation, as former pasture slowly evolves into woodland. And every interaction with these trees – from planning the wood to planting and nurturing them, to recording their progress up close – is a marvellous privilege. In my diary I note the events, both large and small, in the life of the wood: the first time that a tree flowers and sets seed; the appearance in a single season of two years' worth of shoots on an oak tree; and, by mimicking nature's tricks, the small triumph of rescuing a tree that appeared to have died. I share my passion for trees and woods with other local woodland owners, with gardeners and friends; and I teach courses celebrating our enduring relationship with trees and the landscapes they inhabit and create.

From being a field with sticks lost amongst tall grass, Thistle Wood is slowly evolving into something else: an organism in its own right; a self-governing habitat; a small world generating myriad relationships between plant and animal life, subtly altering the shape of the skyline from the moment the first tree rises above head height. A pond, which I dug last autumn to hold water from an old field drain, has already attracted its first damselflies, while the thistles that give the wood its name are buzzing with pollinating bees and butterflies. Newly planted trees are facing the test of the very hot, dry summer of 2018: a few have given up and died and will have to be replaced. It is a dynamic world in action, constantly changing but always sustaining.

The same fascination grips the imagination of school students whose world is constructed of concrete and glass, when a teacher or form group decides to plant acorns or apple pips in a container one autumn, just to see what happens. Schools with playing fields of flat, mown grass are transformed when an area is set aside as a living, outdoor classroom – a small woodland with trees, shade, dappled sunlight, singing birds and busy insects.

A single apple, plum or cherry tree planted in a garden gives lasting pleasure as it matures and bears fruit. A rowan, holly or small clump of hawthorns introduced into a municipal flower bed changes one's relationship with the architecture of road, pavement and apartment block.

Increasingly, communities – of neighbourhoods, schools, social networks and families – are getting together to find ways of planting trees, to foster friendship and collaborative enterprise in gardens and allotments, community woodlands or uncared-for plantations. Worldwide, ever more ambitious schemes are creating new forests on a huge scale to redress imbalances between natural and constructed environments. The Earth needs trees, and so do human societies. Trees can change lives.

An old Chinese proverb says that the best time to plant a tree was twenty years ago; but the next best time is now.

1. WHY PLANT TREES ?

rees are useful. In fact, they are so good at what they do that it is easy to take them for granted. Each individual tree is a complex organism capable of taking up sunlight, water and carbon dioxide and chemically converting these elements into sugars and more sophisticated substances such as lignin and cellulose. Then when a tree dies it becomes an energy asset, releasing calories as it burns or rotting to provide food for invertebrate life. Charcoal – wood burned in a kiln with restricted oxygen – can reinvigorate poor soils and help them to hold more moisture in dry environments, as well as being an effective filter of gases and poisons and the fuel for our garden barbecues. It is the substance that drove early metalworking and the fundamental technological revolutions. Wooden tools and devices and the secret of fire were humans' companions in their cultural evolution. Wood converted to furniture or used as building timber is a long-lasting artistic and engineering investment: biodegradable, strong under tension and compression, adaptable, weather-proof and pleasing to look at and touch.

The living tree is a habitat for all manner of creatures, providing shelter, nesting sites, perches, refuges and frames for climbing. Leaves, bark and sap offer grazing, sugars, fruits and medicines to a host of partners and predators.

Trees enhance landscapes, neighbourhoods, gardens, schools and even the sides of tall buildings. They define skylines, fill valleys and gorges to overflowing, etch boundaries around fields and the sinuous lines of ancient roads. Every species offers something distinct and special, from the graceful rowan standing sentinel by a mountain burn to the soaring Scots pine, the spreading oak and the cathedral-like architecture of a mature beech tree. A wooded landscape is a fine thing to see and travel through, and also to live and work in, but even a single tree planted in a container in a concrete school playground or supermarket car park punches above its weight: it flourishes while all around it is inert and unchanging.

The trees that we plant are a legacy for future generations, just as those ancient ones that we enjoy are a disinterested gift from our ancestors. A tree may stand for a thousand years; its wood may hold a building up for another thousand.

Trees trap pollutants from the atmosphere and give oxygen to our cities. They are tools for the architect and landscape designer; playgrounds for children; models of stability, persistence and stoicism; architects of hope. They bring wildlife and colour into urban spaces, offer an ever-changing view as each season turns, and in the sound of a breeze passing through their branches and leaves there is the echo of a fractured relationship with the lost, ancient wildwood.

Trees that grow in areas of high rainfall and flooding risk slow the passage of water into drains, burns and rivers; they stabilise weak soils and absorb excess moisture from the earth. They blanket the land like thermal insulators, keeping the air cool in summer and mild in winter; they offer shelter and shade in rain and hot sun.

The ancient woodlands of Britain, those continuously present since 1600 or before, are a very special asset in a land that is less wooded than much of the rest of Europe. They preserve an exceptional range of floral and faunal species, while the soils in which they grow are uniquely valuable reserves of precious fungi and microbial life. Ancient woods are records of a sympathetic cultural relationship with nature, a lesson in sustainability and a historian's archive: they can be managed to benefit diversity and continuity, providing at the same time an infinitely sustainable source of fuel, timber, coppice products and – not least – pleasure. They are carbon reserves, air-conditioning systems, soil guardians and installation art combined: the perfect partnership between humans and nature.

Why plant trees when they can reproduce on their own? It is a good question. In any temperate climate, if you fence off an area of moorland or hill pasture to exclude deer, rabbits and sheep, or leave an arable field unploughed for just a few years, it will 'tumble down' to woodland. Birch seeds will arrive on the wind; acorns will be planted by jays and hazelnuts by squirrels; sycamores and maples will helicopter in; and songbirds will drop seeds ready-prepared for germination. Woodland will take over an unfarmed landscape in no time: nature will do its thing. But plant a tree or a small woodland where there was only mown grass or wasteland before; eat apples or plums from your own orchard; fashion a walking stick or a willow basket from a tree that you grew from seed or cutting; sit in the shade of a beech that your grandmother or grandfather planted, and you will experience some of the inestimable joys of growing trees.

2. HOW TREES GROW AND REPRODUCE

Basic tree design

Some plants die after a season's growth and rely on their scattered seeds to return in spring. Others, the perennials, die back then grow again, storing enough energy in their roots to survive the winter months. Trees and other 'woody' plants are defined by their ability to keep each year's growth and build on it, eventually outlasting and outgrowing nearly every other form of life on Earth. They do this by creating an almost-dead skeleton of long, hard, woody vessels called xylem cells, constructed like a spiral staircase and growing outwards as a series of concentric rings with every year's growth. Growing on the outside of the dead xylem, phloem and cambium cells transport water and minerals up the trunk of a tree from its roots to its growing parts (the twigs and leaves) and carry energy, in the form of sugars, back from the leaves to power new growth. The very thin outer layers of cells stretch like skin to allow the trunk to expand inside its bark – the protective outer layer that defends it against weather, animals and disease and through which it breathes.

Leaves are the tree's miraculous power generators: absorbing sunlight and converting it into sugars; transpiring water, exchanging atmospheric carbon dioxide for oxygen and thereby storing the primary greenhouse gas as carbon until the tree dies and the wood rots or is burned. Leaves are held out horizontally in order to catch sunlight by hydraulic pressure – water drawn up from their roots pumps through their tiny veins. In long spells of hot dry weather trees can't usually draw up enough water, through the many miles of vessels in their trunks and branches, to cope with the amount of sunlight their leaves are absorbing, so the millions of tiny pores on the underside of the leaves – the stomata – close, and the leaf becomes limp. In winter, in temperate lands, there is not enough sunlight for normal leaves to function efficiently, and trees – like ships under full sail – are at risk of being capsized by high winds; so the leaves are shed and new buds form to bring fresh growth in spring. The leaves of each tree species are adapted to their own niches: large and waxy to tolerate shade and repel the leaching effects of heavy rain in the tropics; light and aerodynamic in temperate regions. Evergreens, such as pines and spruces, have special narrow leaves called needles and tall, narrow profiles to catch as much winter sunlight as possible so they can keep their dark green foliage for several years, but are able to withstand high winds and the burden of heavy snow. Trees are stressed by extremes of cold and heat, but have evolved extraordinarily effective means of surviving whatever nature can throw at them.

Flowers

Even trees die eventually. Some, like the silver birch, may only live for a hundred years or so. Like animals, trees reproduce sexually (although many have other tricks up their sleeves, too). The reproductive parts of a tree are its flowers, male and female. Some trees are *either* male *or* female (hollies, willows and yews are examples of 'dioecious' trees) while others bear male and female flowers on the same tree (and so are 'monoecious', such as alder, beech, oak and hazelnut).

On some trees the different parts are obvious: catkins on hazelnut trees are the male parts, producing pollen from their stamens; the tiny red female flowers have stigmas that receive fertilising pollen, and they produce seeds and nuts for the next generation. Some flowers contain both male and female parts in one: the so-called 'hermaphrodites', such as cherries and hawthorns. Flowers and seeds cost a great deal of the tree's energy to produce, and the larger and more showy the flower, the more costly it is. These tend to be the flowers that need to attract insect or bird partners to shift their pollen to female flowers on others of their kind. Some flowers are much more subtle: these generally belong to trees that rely on the wind to pollinate them. Most people passing beneath an oak or beech tree in spring, when the first flush of leaves is such a welcome sight, might not notice the yellowy-green flowers hanging down from their twigs. Other species – the hawthorns and rowans, apples and horse chestnuts, for example – produce abundant, highly visible and often sweet-smelling flowers, attracting potential couriers to pass pollen from male to female flowers in exchange for sweet (and costly) nectar.

Pollen

To the naked eye pollen grains are just yellow dust particles, pretty to watch and marvel at as drifting clouds in the still air of spring – unless you happen to be allergic to them. Under a microscope they reveal brilliantly detailed and fantastic architecture that makes each species' pollen uniquely right for the female flower it needs to fertilise.

All trees use one or more partners to carry their pollen from male to female. The early colonisers of the British Isles after the last Ice Age – Scots pines, birches, aspens and willows – relied on wind to shift their pollen around. It seems rather a chance affair, and so it is: but that's why wind-pollinated trees produce so much pollen and also why those species spread out in a direction following the prevailing wind – south-west to north-east in Britain. Generally, trees avoid self-pollination because of the risks of genetic dysfunction. How do they do that? Many trees produce male and female flowers at slightly different times so that the male pollen of one tree is likely only to fertilise the female flowers of another. One of nature's neatest tricks, which slightly raises the odds in favour of pollinating success, is that male and female flowers carry minute positive and negative electrical charges and the shapes of many female flowers create tiny vortices, so pollen passing by on the breeze has a better chance of becoming attached to their stigmas. The showier trees require more active partners: bees are the great pollinators of our gardens and orchards, and they collect pollen both to eat and as a by-product of taking the nectar that the more flashy flowers offer in return for their services. Many other insects act as pollinators, too, as do the smaller birds.

Seeds and fruits

Some trees (including elms, poplars and hollies) are able to spread by sending up suckers from their roots, creating clones of themselves. But for the most part trees rely on producing seeds, in a variety of shapes and sizes, and in all sorts of packages, to spread and sustain their genes.

In native British trees, seeds are generally divided into four types: nuts (technically fruits enclosed in a hard outer casing, such as acorns), winged seeds (maples and hornbeams), those inside fleshy fruits (cherries, rowans and hawthorns) and those in cones (pines, junipers and alders). Trees have evolved many different strategies to give their seeds the best chance to grow successfully. The larger nuts have reserves of fuel that power new shoots and roots ahead of the competition; trees that produce berries raise the odds of spreading their progeny far and wide by engaging birds as partners to carry them away in their stomachs, dispersing them wherever they excrete. Some trees (although none that is native to the British Isles) produce seeds whose germination is triggered by the extreme heat of a forest fire which, literally, kills off the competition. Others, such as the birch, make tiny seeds by the thousand, like confetti. Each seed has a small chance of landing in the right place on bare soil and not being eaten, rotting or ending up flushed into a river. But look at any patch of recently cleared ground, or the edges of a railway embankment, and you'll see how successful is the birch – the greatest coloniser.

The nuts – acorns, beech, walnut, hazel and so on – will germinate in the first spring after some helpful animal or human buries them in a field or in a pot of compost. Winged seeds tend to have built-in dormancy, delaying germination through the winter and early spring so that tender new shoots aren't caught out by a sudden sharp frost. The fleshy fruits – attractive berries and the like – are even more dormant and need special treatment (like the acids in a bird's stomach) plus a period of cold to trigger them.

For each tree a set of rules governs the size, number and distribution of seeds or nuts. The larger the nut or seed-bearing fruit, the more energy is required to make it. Fruit trees, such as apples, pears and plums, invest huge energy in each fruit, in the form of sugar, in the hope of attracting a suitable partner (in the mountains of Kazakhstan, where wild apples first grew, native horses and pigs are the partners in question) who will take the seed away and treat it right, their stomachs stripping it of its dormancy coating and usefully depositing it with a small pile of fertiliser.

Fruit trees produce fewer seeds than, say, the ash, whose bundles of distinctive 'keys' can number in the thousands per tree. The risk of producing fewer, more expensive seeds is that none of them might succeed. The silver birch adopts the opposite strategy, going for small size and great numbers. There is a third way, too: oaks and beeches produce variable numbers of nuts every year. One theory is that their nuts are so attractive to grazing animals (pigs and horses again) that the whole of each year's crop might easily be consumed in one fell swoop. So, once in every few years, the trees produce a massive glut of nuts, as if to say, 'go on, eat that lot if you can'. These periodic gluts are called 'mast' years and the strategy is one of satiation.

3. WHICH TREES TO PLANT, AND WHERE

A note on natives...

The UK supports some thirty-eight native species of tree. There is nothing remotely wrong with planting trees that are not native, in the right place at the right time, but in this book I want to encourage and celebrate the diversity of indigenous species and promote their planting. Some trees, such as the beech, sweet chestnut and sycamore, are either non-native naturalised species, introduced many hundreds or thousands of years ago, or are strictly 'native' only to parts of the island. If you read the literature on this subject you'll find hard-held opinions. Section 4 (page 51) includes a handy list of those trees generally regarded as native.

... and on ash trees

The common ash, one of our great native woodland and hedgerow sights, ought to play a prominent part in any book about planting trees. It is fast-growing, its wood is very strong and supple, it makes terrific fuel and timber and it has a beauty all its own.

Unfortunately, though, because of the infection of many of our native ash population by the deadly fungus *Chalara fraxinea* (ash dieback), this tree cannot now be purchased or grown commercially in the UK. But, as anyone knows who has tried to kill one or stop its seedlings growing anywhere and everywhere in their garden, the ash is not giving up yet. Who can say which specimens or woodlands will prove to be resistant, providing the stock from which to regenerate the dying ash woodlands? My own plantation has two large, mature ash trees which spread their copious offspring everywhere – and when I spot one of these I am careful to protect and nurture it.

So if you can't buy an ash tree for your wood or garden, you can at least let those that arrive under their own steam thrive. However, it is extremely important that if you suspect any of your trees are suffering from ash dieback you deal with it responsibly to prevent it spreading, and report it to the proper authorities: www. forestry.gov.uk/treealert.

Trees for shelter, conservation and landscape

Some trees have a greater impact on the landscape than others; it depends on the species and where you plant them. Fast-growing, thick, bushy trees such as Scots pines or shrubs such as hawthorn provide shelter and privacy for parks, gardens and houses in just a few years.

For landscape value, think of trees both as

individuals, emphasising prominences or hiding industrial structures, and as 'forests', in large plantings with each other or with other species. Even a small clump of trees can make a significant difference to a landscape in need of interest, habitat diversity or protection. All native trees offer habitats, shelter and food for the insects, lichens, birds and mammals that have evolved with them over millennia. Sufficiently large woodlands located carefully in areas prone to flooding absorb groundwater, stabilise soils and slow down rainwater runoff, giving rivers and meadows the chance to naturally maintain safe water levels.

The grandest landscape trees, given the room to really show off their potential, are the oaks and ashes, beeches, Scots pines, limes and elms. You might not appreciate them until they are gone. Planting these wonderful trees in hedgerow or woodland, park or garden is a gift to a future generation. Although young elms remain a common sight in our hedgerows, mature elms are no longer a feature of the countryside: they are prone to attack from the elm bark beetle and are especially vulnerable because many elms reproduce by suckers, restricting their genetic diversity and resistance.

Trees for fruit and nuts

There is no reason why trees shouldn't be productive. Fruit trees in all their variety (many thousands of cultivars are available) are well worth planting. Consult your local tree nursery or a specialist supplier for the best examples to grow in your area and think about trying something out of the ordinary, like a damson.

Every spring, supermarkets sell fruit trees cheaply and in bulk – they are perhaps not the greatest specimens, but plant a few and the chances are that many will take and produce apples, plums, cherries and pears. Or for something different, there are several varieties of hazelnut – cobs and filberts, for example – and the hazelnut, along with the seeds of Scots pines, is the preferred food of our native and endangered red squirrel. All fruit trees are great for attracting pollinators into the garden and for encouraging children to eat fruit and understand where it comes from.

All these trees can be propagated at home, and it's great fun to try growing them from seed, cutting or graft (see Section 5, page 87, for the basics). The pips from a favourite apple, incidentally, are most unlikely to produce a tree of the same variety – apples are heterozygous, meaning that their genes are mixed up in reproduction. Your Cox's Orange Pippin pip might grow into a tree with fruits that are too sharp to eat; it might also grow into a tree that produces the best-tasting apple ever; but it's most unlikely to produce a true Cox's Orange Pippin.

Trees for timber, fuel or making things

Few projects give more satisfaction than growing trees to use as fuel or to make things. From the simple cut hazel rod for a walking stick or garden support, to pines, oaks and beech for construction, furniture, carving and all types of timber for wood burners, cutting wood from trees that you have grown is immensely gratifying. And it's never too late to start – in ten years you could be fuel-self-sufficient from scratch.

Hazels are traditionally 'coppiced' (cut down to the ground, then they rapidly shoot again with renewed vigour, producing multiple straight stems) every seven or eight years; ash and beech every twelve to fifteen years and oaks after about twenty years. Good trees for fuel include beech and oak, all fruit woods (which give off a divine aroma on an open fire), birch, sycamore and Scots pine. Fast-growing willow is now often planted as a commercial fuel crop. It is generally thought that to be completely self-sufficient in fuel wood for a family home you would need about 2.5 hectares (7 acres) of trees. An acre should produce a ton of new wood every year; cut each acre on a seven-year cycle and you'll be able to harvest 7 tonnes per year – for ever. But with modern lean-burn stoves about 4–5 tonnes should easily provide most of the heat for a home. I have often built wood stores from my own timber, doubling the satisfaction. There's an old saying that wood warms you three times: once when you cut it, once when you stack it, and finally when you burn it. I can vouch for that.

Trees for gardens

Rowan, guelder rose, crab apple, hawthorn and blackthorn make fine garden trees individually or as small woodland copses, offering foliage, flowers, berries and visual interest all year round.

For bigger gardens, silver birch, whitebeam, yew and field maple will give form, colour, a third dimension and architectural interest.

Even modest-sized gardens can have a woody area of small trees, underplanted with woodland flowers to create a sense of intimacy and a more relaxed side of nature. Woods are cool in the heat of summer and retain a milder temperature than open land in winter; and they provide a haven for all sorts of birds, amphibians, insects and small mammals, creating a special ecosystem of their own. A clump of trees also makes a perfect play area for children to express their imagination and sense of freedom and wonder. Add a wildlife pond and you will be doing hard-pressed nature a small but significant favour.

There is no reason at all why you shouldn't plant one or more of the many available cultivars and exotic trees in your garden. There are some wonderful maples that bring stupendous autumn colour and very pretty foliage, while fruit trees now come in myriad varieties, such as the logan-berry and medlar, which can be grown against a sunny wall in the garden of a terraced house or in a patio container. I've even seen a Ginkgo tree grown in a pot, and there are floating gardens with small trees on the River Thames and on the canals of the Midlands and in Northern England. Your local nursery or garden centre will advise on suitable trees depending on your garden's aspect, local climate and soil conditions, but it's also worth experimenting. Swapping cuttings or grafts with neighbours or local friends is a great way to share knowledge and beautiful plants. Many communities now have very active plant-swapping events.

Trees for hedges

The best trees for hedges are those that respond well to coppicing (repeated cutting every few years), including hazel, hawthorn, hornbeam, blackthorn, elm, holly, field maple and beech. A thick, dense hedge can be grown from scratch in a very few years, providing a windbreak, seasonal visual interest and rich habitats for nesting birds, insects and small mammals. Planting a small hedged area in a garden creates a cherished private space in which to enjoy the outdoors.

Many suppliers offer varieties of hedging packs at relatively little cost. Hedges are easily planted and, so long as they are maintained and any lost plants are replaced, will last a lifetime and longer. Maintain a hedge by trimming it regularly – or, even better, by 'laying' it using traditional techniques and materials, helping to preserve an ancient and valuable craft. (See under hawthorn and blackthorn for planting instructions in Section 4, page 66.) The Tree Council produces *The Hedge Tree Handbook* (see Further reading, page 167) for more information.

Planning a new wood

Small woods are ecologically important as refuges for wildlife, linking wider habitats and creating their own. There is no minimum size for a wood: even a quarter of an acre, once planted and established, will give a sense of woodland intimacy and mystery as well as providing fuel, nuts, berries and year-round interest. Woodland classics such as oak, elm, beech, hazel, cherry and rowan, alders and willows for damper areas and crab apple, hawthorn and blackthorn for flowers and berries will all establish within a few years.

In planning a new woodland it is important, but not easy, to visualise how it will look in the future. Creating rides – the tracks that weave between trees – is crucial: in fact, the more the better, especially when they run east to west. The south-facing side of these rides soaks up the sun and, when properly managed in successive layers from the ground up (flowers, small bushes, larger bushes, then full-grown trees), it becomes a key micro-habitat in a wood. Mark out generous rides at least 5 metres (16 ft) wide and try to make them curvy for ever-renewing views. Think about the visual impact of trees where rides and paths meet – I always like to grow something individual and striking, such as a rowan, holly or Scots pine.

Take advantage of even small features on the land – humps and bumps or gentle shallow valleys. Prominent trees planted on higher ground offer greater visual impact. It might seem odd to say this, but small clearings, or glades, in woods are also important, creating varied habitats that will be colonised by wild flowers and birds.

Make sure that on exposed edges (normally to the west) you plant robust trees that can take strong winds, and plant them more densely here to improve storm protection for the rest of the trees. Scots pines are very useful, as fast-growing bushy trees, for creating windbreaks, and so too are the hedge species hawthorn, blackthorn and dog rose. Try to plan for the future; in due course it will be worth replacing some taller trees of the same age with new, younger plants, to ensure a mixed, sustainable structure for the long term.

Community planting

One hears encouraging tales of communities that have raised the funds to purchase, or have otherwise acquired, plots of land of all sizes on which to plant trees. Community woods that involve lots of people across various ages and backgrounds in their development, management and conservation are surely assets well worth the social and financial investment from people whose sense of belonging might be based on living in a street, village or town.

Woodlands are not only more beneficial to people when their pleasures and products are shared, but also when the investments of labour and emotional energy are collaborative. Equipment can be owned in partnership, with skills acquired and shared and schools involved, so that a social asset is enjoyed across the community. Sometimes local councils are happy for groups to take on scraps of untended land, while even private individuals may be keen to see a piece of land become productive. For anyone interested, there is a Community Woodland Association in Scotland that provides support, advice and encouragement; and across the UK the Woodland Trust runs a Community Woodland network (see Useful information, page 161, for details).

Trees for schools
(small and large, rural or urban)

Even the most urban school, where every inch of earth is covered by paving or concrete, will benefit from growing trees. Either create a bed by removing the ground covering and working the soil, or plant in recycled containers – try planters made from stacks of rubber tyres, or nail together some railway sleepers or old pallets. As long as trees are well watered and cared for, they can thrive in the smallest spaces. Pollution-resistant trees are particularly good for cities, especially the field maple and several of the willows, which are very fast-growing and extremely easy to propagate. Fruit trees will provide endless interest for pupils, parents and teachers. Even better, plant a hedge along a playing field boundary and establish an outdoor woodland classroom. Get children to plant seeds and take cuttings; the Woodland Trust gives away large numbers of free trees to schools (see Useful information on page 161). As a fundraising project to get parents, communities and sponsors involved, tree propagation and planting – even on a small scale – offers multiple benefits for schools. You could even establish a nursery and raise funds by selling seedlings. I know of schools that keep beehives and make their own honey, too.

For smaller spaces I recommend rowan, white-beam, guelder rose and well-pruned fruit trees, holly and field maple; for larger areas, try birch, rowan, beech, oak, holly and Scots pine, and willows for willow tunnels or domes. Or why not plant one or more of the less well-known natives: walnut, black poplar, yew, small-leaved lime or wild service tree? And there are some wonderful, often neglected fruit trees, too, such as damson, quince and mulberry.

The outdoor classroom

Some schools are reluctant to plant trees or allow wildness in, partly for the sake of tidiness and partly because of a fear of maintenance costs or health and safety. But there's no reason why pupils themselves shouldn't be taught how to trim or lay a hedge, coppice their trees and learn how to protect them, in the process acquiring skills, a sense of ownership and an understanding of how to safely use tools under adult supervision. Pupils can learn how to stack and season logs and safely light fires. A small bonfire provides an atmospheric place in which to learn and tell stories together, or just to be quiet, to watch and listen.

As outdoor classrooms in all seasons of the year, woody areas provide a sense of intimacy and magic, are full of science, maths, art and English lessons as well as being places to exercise and let off steam. Schools with wild areas have healthier pupils.* The outdoor classroom can give pupils of any age an enriching learning experience. Forest schools are an increasingly popular way of getting pupils out of the four walls of a classroom and into an exciting world of nature. Why not bring the forest into your school? I would suggest relieving parental fears about scratched and muddy uniforms by getting each pupil a set of

* https://www.nationaltrust.org.uk/documents/read-our-natural-childhood-report.pdf

cheap overalls and wellies, so they can get really, properly dirty without being told off when they get home.

A note on ponds

Even a small pond provides a fascinating and beautiful focus among trees, offering a haven for insects and amphibians and a drinking hole for birds and small mammals. Put a bench next to a pond in a partially shaded woody area and you may find yourself spending many happy hours doing nothing but watching and listening. Place a movement-triggered camera nearby and you'll see how many creatures take advantage of your generosity. I'm amazed at how many feathered parents bring their young to my woodland pond to teach them how to take a bath. And it doesn't take long for a pond to attract new residents. During the first spring at my new pond, damselflies and dragonflies turned up in abundance, along with pond skaters and freshwater snails. Frogs and toads are sure to follow.

I have planted native water-loving flowers – flag iris, water mint, loosestrife, waterlilies and others – to keep the water of my new pond cool, clear and healthy. Alders, rowans and willows thrive in damp places and furnish a pond with useful shade. There are many good books and plenty of online advice on how to build and look after a wildlife pond (see Further reading, page 167).

4. SOME BRITISH NATIVES FOR PLANTING

For propagation and planting advice, see Section 5 (page 87).

Silver birch (*Betula pendula*) and downy birch (*Betula pubescens*)

There are two native species of the slender birch: the well-known silver birch, with its creamy white papery bark, and the downy birch, whose bark is more variably brown and whose leaves have tiny soft hairs. The unshowy cousin, downy birch is a tough dweller of hillsides and damp areas. The more commonly planted silver birch is a tall, elegant tree that casts light shade, tolerates poor soils and is a rapid coloniser of waste or newly bare earth. It comes alive with the sound of a summer breeze and sways dramatically in a storm. The leaves are small and pale green with serrated edges, turning yellow in autumn, and when they fall they create very little leaf litter. Birches are monoecious, producing both male and female catkins on the same tree.

All birches are cold-adapted, which means that in response to very hard frosts, they charge their roots with positive hydraulic pressure in early spring, forcing sap up the trunk to expel damaging pockets of air in their vessels. As a result these trees produce a sticky sweet sap that can be tapped to make a drink (the maple trees of North America make use of the same mechanism, producing their prized syrup). Birches will grow to a height of more than 20 metres (66 ft). They do not respond particularly well to coppicing and usually live to no more than about 100 years. Even so, they grow quickly, providing an early structural and sheltering element for a new plantation or garden without dominating or shading out other plants. It is possible to buy young trees of about 1.2 metres (4 ft) in height for a couple of pounds each, but it is also very easy to grow birch trees by sprinkling the seed (you can hold thousands in the palm of one hand) collected in early autumn by rubbing the catkins between your fingers, onto moist bare soil or compost covered with a thin topping of sharp sand (it is slightly acidic and easy to obtain from a garden centre or hardware shop).

Hazelnut (*Corylus avellana*)

This is a much under-rated small tree, and one that has been a staple of British woodlands for thousands of years because of its nuts and the large number of products it yields when coppiced regularly. It was, like the birch, one of the early colonisers of the British Isles after the last Ice Age, its nuts perhaps originally brought in by nomadic hunter-gatherer groups. The oldest house ever to be excavated in England by archaeologists, at Howick, in Northumberland, showed that its inhabitants were keen hazelnut eaters more than 8,000 years ago.

If you cut down a hazelnut tree to just above ground level a couple of years after planting, it will sprout vigorously with several new, straight shoots. After that it can be cut every seven or eight years to produce a regular crop of rods for garden stakes, fencing hurdles and many more useful items. I sometimes call it the walking stick tree, and I often cut myself a stick when out and about - it does the tree no harm at all. In fact, the hazelnut tree is self-coppicing: it will throw up new shoots of its own accord. It is hardy and grows in most soils and its shoots will grow 60–90 centimetres (2–3 ft) per year when established; but the tree never gets much taller than about 7 metres (23 ft). The leaves are large, veined and roundish, with a pointed tip; the stems speckled brown. Buds form on opposite sides of the shoots and can be pinkish just before they burst. One of the loveliest but most subtle signs of spring, when the hazelnut is laden with fresh yellow catkins but has not yet produced leaves, is the appearance of minute red florets on its stems: the female flowers.

Hazelnut wood is good as a fuel crop and for fencing and hedging materials, while the living trees make fine hedges in their own right. Plant seedlings in the autumn and give them full sun to encourage nut production. They are easy to grow from nuts collected in autumn - look for the yellowy bracts, like old-fashioned hats, that give the nut and the tree their Old English name, *hæsl*, meaning 'cap' - and cheap to buy as hedging plants. For propagation see 'Nuts' and 'Cuttings and layering' in Section 5. Several cultivated hybrids offer abundant nut crops.

Oak (*Quercus robur* and *Quercus petraea*)

There are two species of native British oak: pedunculate (*Quercus robur*) and sessile (*Quercus petraea*). The former bears its acorns on long stalks while the leaves have short stalks, whereas in sessile oaks the opposite is true. The two species also hybridise. Both are keystones of our native woods, providing the richest range of habitats for invertebrates, birds and mammals. Oaks are extremely long-lived – several hundred years at least – and can be encouraged to live even longer by coppicing or pollarding.

You need a large garden to think about planting oaks but, as Admiral Collingwood recommended (see Section 8, page 144), you can always pop an acorn or two into a bare-looking hedgerow and see what happens. If you do have the space to plant oaks, it couldn't be easier to grow them. Just do what jays do every autumn: collect fresh acorns as they fall from a tree and prod them into the ground with a stick to a depth of about 4 centimetres (1.5 in.) – see Section 5, 'Nuts' (page 99).

Oaks were traditionally used not just for their fine, strong timber in house- and ship-building, but to preserve and soften animal hides in the tanning process (the tannin-rich bark was peeled from a freshly felled tree in early summer before the trunk was sawn into planks) and for charcoal making. The galls attached to oaks by wasps, and in which they lay their larvae, were crushed and dissolved to make a dark-black, very long-lasting ink, which was used in manuscripts such as the *Lindisfarne Gospels*. Oak trees are late into leaf, produce droops of green flowers in spring and, in 'mast' years, enormous crops of acorns. When under attack from plagues of ants the trees release the vaporous toxic tannin into the air; this drifts towards other oaks, which respond by producing more tannin in their leaves, thus deterring the predatory insects. The trees are, if you like, talking to each other. In extreme circumstances oaks can shed an entire crop of leaves while under attack from insects, then grow another in the same season.

Beech (*Fagus sylvatica*)

A mature beech tree is too large for most gardens. It is greedy for light and water, shade-tolerant and fast-growing. A magnificent sight at all times of the year, its spring leaves are a shiny, translucent emerald green with tiny hairs. The pen-nib buds are distinctive in winter and the muscular grey, smooth trunks are like the soaring columns of a cathedral. For gardens, the beech nevertheless makes a superb hedge, growing densely and keeping many of its dry, brown leaves throughout the winter. If you have the room for a tree, grow a beech or two. New seedlings will grow to about 25 centimetres (10 in.) in their first year, then accelerate as the roots develop. Seedlings can be bought specifically for hedging, although they'll grow into large trees if allowed or encouraged. The tree responds well to coppicing.

As a fuel, the wood from beech trees burns very hot and makes excellent charcoal. The wood is easily worked, turns well on a lathe, and its attractive grain means it is good for use in furniture making. Beech wood was once used to make covers for manuscripts - the word 'book' is derived from the Old English word '*boc*' for the tree. Beech trees have graced the British landscape for at least two thousand years, although there is some dispute about whether they are true natives in the north. The small nuts are very good to eat, too, and the medieval practice of pannage - turning pigs into the woods in autumn to feed on the bounteous mast of oak and beech trees - was responsible for fattening many a porker.

Beech trees are gregarious - that is, they thrive in each other's company. That's because below ground their roots share a relationship with tiny mycorrhizal fungi that they feed with sugar in return for nitrogen and phosphorus. Oddly enough, considering their size when mature, beech trees rarely live beyond 150–200 years. They are easy to grow from their nuts, which in a so-called 'mast year' are produced in vast numbers. Check the shiny brown casing to see if there's a nut inside and plant two or three per pot of compost (see Section 5, 'Nuts', page 99).

Rowan (*Sorbus aucuparia*)

The lovely and delicate rowan, often also known as the mountain ash – even though the two species are unrelated – has inspired poets to versify and storytellers to credit it with magical powers and sacred significance. It will never grow to more than about 15 metres (50 ft) in height and is suitable for many gardens – it can even be cultivated in a container, where it will grow more slowly and can be pruned to a modest size and shape. Rowans produce white flowers in spring and red or orange berries in autumn, when its feathery leaves, looking like the wing tips of soaring raptors, can turn brilliant orange and purple.

Rowan coppices readily, often growing with multiple trunks naturally; and even though it is not cultivated for its timber, the wood will burn well when seasoned. The berries are full of vitamin C and can be made into a jelly; they also provide valuable winter food for birds, especially waxwings. Before the seeds will germinate they must pass through a bird's stomach, where digestive acids strip away the outer dormancy coating. Rowans can be propagated by mimicking this process, called 'stratifying' (see Section 5, 'Fleshy fruits', page 101). This technique does not guarantee results – I must admit that I have had little success with them – but it costs little to try, and the satisfaction of growing such a beautiful tree from seed collected in autumn more than compensates for earlier failure and the effort required.

I plant rowans at strategic points in my plantation, especially where two tracks or rides meet: grown in front of a dark-leaved tree like holly or Scots pine they stand out wonderfully well at all times of the year. A relative of the rowan, the whitebeam (*Sorbus aria*), which has distinctive lobed leaves with a whitish underside and bright autumn berries, is often used in planting schemes on new housing developments. Whitebeams are pollution-resistant and, when well-watered for a couple of years after planting, a line of them creates a leafy and pretty frame for a street.

Wild cherry or gean (*Prunus avium*) and bird cherry (*Prunus padus*)

Cherries are among the very first trees into leaf in spring, providing longed-for bright greenery; and they produce plenty of blossom, so they are valued for parks and gardens. Many cultivars are grown especially for fruit production, too. The bark is a shiny purple-brown with horizontal scabby lines – these are lenticels, pores through which the tree exchanges gases with the atmosphere.

Cherry trees may grow to a substantial height and, with a long straight trunk and dense dark wood, they are prized for their timber and for fuel. They will coppice readily. Cherries are hermaphrodites, with male and female parts in the same flower. The sweet juicy fruits are eaten and dispersed by birds, badgers, dormice and other small mammals – and by humans. Cherries also reproduce by suckers sent out from their roots, so a line of cherry trees might be clones of a single parent. The foliage is the main food plant for caterpillars of many species of moth, including the cherry fruit and cherry bark moths, the orchard ermine, brimstone and short-cloaked moth. Bird cherry trees are distinctive for their candelabra-like white blossoms and less shiny leaves. For propagation advice, see Section 5, 'Fleshy fruits' (page 101).

Hawthorn (*Crataegus monogyna*) and blackthorn (*Prunus spinosa*)

The two most common thorn trees in the British Isles, although they might never grow to the magnificent heights of the oak and beech, these punch well above their weight for impact and value. They are well known as vigorous hedging plants: the springtime white or pinkish blossoms (those of the hawthorn are commonly known as May flowers) are profuse and aromatic, a glory of the British countryside, and their red haws or black sloes are beloved of cattle, birds and, in the case of the latter, sloe gin-makers. Both species bear sharp thorns: those of the hawthorn in particular can create very unpleasant swellings when handled, so I always use gloves when planting or pruning them. Hawthorn leaves are like miniature maple leaves, tightly serrated; those of the blackthorn are smooth and oval.

When grown as hedging plants thorns should be planted in double rows, each plant 40 centimetres (16 in.) from the next in line and offset from a second row 20 centimetres (8 in.) away, so that the planted seedlings form a zig-zag line, each plant about 20 centimetres (8 in.) from its nearest neighbour. This will produce a thick, impenetrable hedge that is perfect for shelter, privacy, livestock enclosure and for nesting birds and scurrying mammals. Each seedling should be protected by a rabbit spiral and cane for a few years until established. I like to mix these two with briar rose and field maple; and it's always nice to have a holly or two in a hedge for visual impact.

Oddly enough, considering its modest size, hawthorn is a much-mentioned tree in historical sources, providing many ancient place names and often included in boundary clauses as a parish or township marker. Many folk tales and superstitions are also told about the hawthorn. The idea that bringing May blossom into a house is unlucky is likely to derive from the chemical that the flowers produce as they decay. It's called triethylamine, and is reminiscent of the smell of rotting flesh and other unmentionable body fluids. Anyone who walks beside a hawthorn hedge in late May will become immediately aware of this distinctive smell.

I cannot speak for blackthorn, but hawthorn makes very good firewood: hard and dense and giving off a robust whiff that evokes cold starlit winter nights. Because it grows in multiple and rarely straight stems, there are few known uses for hawthorn wood in turning or joinery. Blackthorn rods make very good walking sticks and in Ireland they were traditionally cut with a knobbly end to make a distinctly handy weapon, the shillelagh, fashioned to shape and then 'cured' with butter and the peaty smoke of a chimney.

For propagation advice see 'Fleshy fruits' in Section 5 (page 101).

Willows

Bay willow (*Salix pentandra*), crack willow (*Salix fragilis*), goat willow (*Salix caprea*), grey willow (*Salix cinerea*), osier willow (*Salix viminalis*) and white willow (*Salix alba*)

No fewer than six – perhaps more – species of willow are native to the British Isles and they are tricky to tell apart. What they share in common is fast growth, bendy shoots, tolerance of damp places and the remarkable ability of cuttings, or twigs broken off in high winds, to 'strike' or take root without any treatment. Their bark is rich in salicylic acid, the active ingredient of the drug aspirin, first marketed in 1899.

The best way to tell the willows apart is to collect leaves and compare them, with a good tree guide to hand – even so, it takes a while to master their sometimes subtle differences, especially since there are numerous hybrids and cultivars. Goat willow and grey willow are distinctive in spring when they produce the soft, furry, grey catkins that give them the popular name 'pussy willow', and they both have pronounced oval leaves. Crack willow has the odd property that its twigs snap easily when bent – hence the name. Osier willow, often pollarded (cut at about head height) along river banks, its thin shoots or withies used for basket weaving, produces the longest, thinnest, most pointed of the *Salix spp.* leaves.

Willows are widely planted for ornament, for flood defence and for their withies. White willow cultivars are pollarded and their timber is highly prized in the manufacture of cricket bats. All willows will readily coppice, and if you plant two parallel lines of them you can train willows into a tunnel shape that children will love to play in. There's no need to buy a willow tree: they are very easy indeed to propagate from cuttings (see Section 5, 'Cuttings and layering', page 102). The rather unshowy goat willow, which grows as a large shrub, is of high ecological importance as a source of food for butterflies and moth caterpillars, while its catkins buzz with pollinators in spring. Willows are generally dioecious – that is, the trees are either male or female. Their flowers are mostly wind-pollinated.

Holly (*Ilex aquifolium*)

The native holly is an unmistakable icon of countryside, park and garden. It is an evergreen broadleaf (not quite a contradiction in terms) and comes as either a male or female ('dioecious') tree. The male trees produce pollen and the female trees bear flowers that, when pollinated, turn into the bright red berries of autumn so beloved of Christmas wreaths and hungry blackbirds.

Hollies, like other broadleaf trees (and unlike conifers), will happily regrow after being coppiced or heavily pruned. The wood is very smooth, dense and white, turns beautifully on a lathe and has often been used to make chess pieces and candlesticks. The leaves are shiny, dark green and waxy, and on lower branches they are prickly as a deterrent against browsing livestock. Hollies are worth establishing as hedging trees, as individual specimens in gardens for their dramatic year-round effect, and in woodlands, where the berries are a good source of winter food and the dense foliage shelters birds.

The impact of holly trees in the landscape is attested by the common Old English place name element '*holm*'. Like the yew tree, the holly carries ancient symbolic connotations of eternal life (its evergreen leaves) and sacrifice (the blood red of the berries). Sometimes I will find a self-seeded holly sapling in the garden: I lift it carefully to keep all the roots intact and pot it up, watching carefully for a while so that it doesn't get too dry, then plant it out the following autumn. Hollies can be grown from seed (see Section 5, 'Fleshy fruits', page 101); when they come ready-potted from the nursery they are expensive to buy, so it's worth trying to propagate them as hardwood cuttings (see Section 5, 'Cuttings and layering', page 102).

Alder (*Alnus glutinosa*)

People don't plant the common alder in their gardens. If you want to see one, go down to a river or stream bank, or a boggy patch of ground, where they thrive. Often you will see them with three or more trunks – the result of coppicing at some time in the past. Their unpopularity as an ornamental tree probably comes from the inverted cone shape of the mature tree, and from the shovel-like leaves and open canopy they produce. In autumn they do not dazzle with colour: the leaves turn brown and shrivel – the alder is not one of nature's lookers.

Yet these trees are invaluable, not just because they thrive in wet conditions, which makes them ideal for flood risk areas and hilly terrain, but because they are also, like the silver birch, a pioneer species, ready to move into new ground as soon as the opportunity arises. The tree forms a partnership with a nitrogen-fixing bacterium (*Frankia alni*), which means that, like legumes, alders increase the natural fertility of the soil in which they grow, preparing it for other, fussier trees. Alders can grow quickly and make good starter trees for a new woodland plantation, but they need protecting from deer and rabbits, who have a taste for the sweet sap just beneath the bark. The wood is hard, burns well and was once a favourite of the charcoal burner. Alders produce catkins and very distinctive seed cones that stay on the tree through the winter, making them easy to identify. The cones are prized by aquarium owners because they release nitrogen and phosphorous to feed aquatic plants, and contain anti-fungal tannins that keep water clean. For propagating alders from seed, see 'Cones' in Section 5, page 102.

Scots pine (*Pinus sylvestris*)

There are few more majestic sights than a lofty Scots pine tree, its reddish, scaly bark brilliantly lit by a setting sun, its cloud of feathery needle-laden branches deep rich green against a blue sky framed by snow-capped hills. In spring the tree produces clouds of yellow pollen; in high summer its scent is musky and sweet.

This is the UK's only native pine, forming great natural forests in its Caledonian heartlands and, to a lesser extent, on the sandy soils of East Anglia, but working equally well in plantations, parks and gardens. Despite its size it is a discreet tree – its roots won't pull your house down. The timber, once known to carpenters as 'deal', is excellent, valuable for furniture and construction, and the wood burns well in a stove. The Scots pine also provides a rich habitat for small mammals and invertebrates and the seeds are a vital source of food for the native red squirrel and pine marten. Often, in windier parts of the countryside, a belt of these trees betrays the sheltered leeward presence of a farm; elsewhere its natural genetic variety comes out in fantastic twisted forms.

The Scots pine is a gregarious tree, enjoying the proximity of others of the same species whose roots share a relationship with beneficial mycorrhizal fungi below ground. It is relatively easy to grow from seed, which it produces abundantly in cones that grow from the female flowers at the tips of new shoots (see 'Cones' in Section 5, page 102).

Yew (*Taxus baccata*)

The yew is Europe's longest-lived tree, and most of the really ancient specimens are to be found in the medieval churchyards of the British Isles – although no one knows quite why. There are outstanding examples in Perthshire, on Runnymede Island in the River Thames, and in St Cynog's Church in Defynnog, Powys – all of which may be over 2,000 years old. It is not easy to estimate or measure the age of a yew, though; the trees naturally grow with multiple stems (like the hawthorn and rowan) and, in any case, after about their 400th birthday they tend to become hollow, making it difficult to count the annual growth rings.

Considering its great longevity, the yew can grow remarkably quickly in its early years, with thick, rich, dark green needles looking quite like those of a pine tree. It bears very striking red arils – the fleshy seed casings that are so attractive to birds. But all parts of the yew (except the red flesh of the aril) are very poisonous, so it is not suitable for an area where young children play. Like the evergreen holly, the yew has often been associated with sacrifice and the everlasting, which is why traditionally a yew log – the Yule log – was brought into the home during Christmas to burn, marking the shortest day and the sun's renewal at the winter solstice.

The wood has a wonderfully rich and smooth grain and, just where the heartwood meets the outer sapwood, its combined strength and flexibility made yew the prize timber for carving medieval longbows. Yews make very good dense hedging and have often been used in the construction of mazes, and they make a striking addition to a garden, park or square. New trees can be grown from seed (see Section 5, 'Fleshy fruits', page 101) but they may take at least two years of stratifying (see Section 5, 'Winged seeds', page 100) before they germinate.

Field maple (*Acer campestre*)

There is only one native maple, and it is the least ostentatious of the lot. It doesn't often grow much bigger than a rowan and in hedges it is often mistaken for the hawthorn, whose leaves are similar in shape, if smaller. But take a closer look at a field maple and it comes into its own. The fresh spring leaves flush with a lovely red wine colour before they turn green. They grow on reddish stalks in tight clusters from branches with an odd, distinctive corky bark. The flowers come out in April and May and their yellow-green colour is a clue that the field maple is primarily wind-pollinated.

These trees will grow almost anywhere, are pollution-resistant and can take quite a bit of grazing from horses and cattle – so they are ideal hedging plants. Their paired seeds look like smaller versions of the sycamore 'helicopters' beloved of children. They are not known as a commercial timber tree, but the attractive red wood is hard enough to use for tool handles. Hedging aside, they make terrific garden trees with colourful autumn foliage and can be pruned into compact, bushy shapes. For propagation information, see 'Winged seeds' in Section 5, page 100.

Fruit and nut trees and bushes

Orchards are a great glory of the landscape. Apart from their very evident productivity and visual attractions, they are vitally important for sustaining pollinating insects. Even a single productive tree in a school, park or garden is better than none. Many fruit trees are self-pollinating – that is to say, they don't need another tree of the same or similar variety to set seed and produce fruit. Others – apples are the best-known – do require pollinating partners; but it's very easy to buy two apple trees of the right pollination groups from a local nursery: ask for advice if you're not sure.

The native crab apple (*Malus sylvestris*: see below) is the rootstock on which most, if not all, commercial apple cuttings are grafted as 'scions'.

It is an important tree in its own right, providing food for birds and mammals deep into winter and offering abundant nectar in spring. Fruit woods are generally hard and oily and were traditionally used to make the teeth in mill gears, for they are both tough and self-lubricating. For the propagation of fruit trees, see Section 5, 'Grafting' (page 104).

Generally woodland trees and orchard trees are kept discreetly separate; but I am very taken by the work of the Forest Garden movement (see Further reading, page 167), in which a more natural, productive role for trees is a key principle. In a woodland the edges of the rides are regarded as the most dynamic and richest habitats. A ride of about 8–12 metres (26–40 ft) wide, whose south-facing edge rises gradually from the woodland floor to the tree canopy, is the perfect place to encourage woodland produce. Here I start with strawberries, currants, gooseberries and soft fruit bushes such as raspberries (wild or cultivated), then come fruit and nut trees: apples, cherries, plums, cobs and filberts (varieties of cultivated hazelnuts), then the larger trees for coppicing or growing to full height. The result is a terrace of layers benefiting from shelter and sunlight that are productive and attractive to a large variety of birds, mammals and invertebrates and make an enriching space in which to walk and contemplate the passing of the seasons.

Britain's other native trees: a challenge

Why not try to plant and grow a specimen of each of the native trees of the British Isles? A medium-sized school or a large garden could easily accommodate all thirty-eight of these or so, to make a wonderful collection from which children can learn about tree biology and adaptation, ecological history and the practical skills of planting and nurturing.

The following is a list of the other native trees that have not been fully described above.

- **Box** (*Buxus sempervirens*): often seen as topiary or as a closely pruned hedge.
- **Midland hawthorn** (*Crataegus laevigata*): a now-rare cousin of the common hawthorn.
- **Hornbeam** (*Carpinus betulus*): widely coppiced in southern England for its very hard wood and commonly seen as a planted hedge, it has leaves similar to those of beech but more ribbed. Its seeds are distinctively triple-winged, like birds' feet.
- **Spindle** (*Euonymus europaeus*): a large bush of hedgerows, with distinctive pink flowers.
- **Ash** (*Fraxinus excelsior*): cannot now be planted because of the deadly *Chalara fraxinea* fungus but self-seeds abundantly. Winged seeds.
- **Juniper** (*Juniperus communis*): one of three native conifers, low-growing, now increasingly rare; produces berries (strictly speaking, cones) used in flavouring gin.

- **Crab apple** (*Malus sylvestris*): our native apple; a valuable source of pollen for bees as well as fleshy fruit for birds and mammals, used as stock for grafting apple cultivars. Will grow from seed.

- **White poplar** (*Populus alba*): a very fast-growing, tall tree which produces abundant suckers; unsuitable for gardens.

- **Black poplar** (*Populus nigra*): a magnificent but endangered native woodland tree. Grown from cuttings.

- **Aspen** (*Populus tremula*): a tall tree of damp places with trembling foliage. Grown from cuttings.

- **Plymouth pear** (*Pyrus cordata*): very rare; it bears small, round fleshy fruit.

- **Buckthorn** (*Rhamnus cathartica*): a bush of scrubby woods, with black berries.

- **Elder** (*Sambucus nigra*): a shrubby tree of hedgerows and gardens with exuberant, aromatic cream flower clusters and bright black autumn berries. Grown from seed.

- **Wild service tree** (*Sorbus torminalis*): rare, highly

distinctive tree with maple-like leaves and small pear-shaped fruit.

+ **Common lime** (*Tilia* x *europaea*): a large, elegant tree with heart-shaped leaves; commonly sends up new shoots from its base.

+ **Small-leaved lime** (*Tilia cordata*): a frequently coppiced tree in medieval woods. Fleshy fruits.

+ **Large-leaved lime** (*Tilia platyphyllos*): the rarest of its native cousins.

+ **Wych elm** (*Ulmus glabra*): a large, once-common tree with distinctive flat yellow seed cases that can be collected in summer and planted immediately.

+ **Guelder rose** (*Viburnum opulus*): a pretty shrub of hedge and woodland edge with bright red trans-lucent berries.

5. PLANTING AND PROPAGATION

Planting a tree:
two basic methods

When you buy a tree it will generally be delivered either bare-rooted (if ordering in the winter months) or in a pot. I always soak bare-rooted trees in rainwater for at least 24 hours before I plant them: most planting failures are caused by allowing the roots to dry out. I always try to plant on a dull, mizzly day with little or no breeze, too, so that the roots are not exposed to a drying wind. Autumn is best for planting: there is little risk of frost and trees get a chance to bed in while more or less dormant, so that they are stressed as little as possible. I carry saplings around in a large bag (they are usually delivered in tied batches with their roots in a plastic bag) and leave them inside right up to the moment of planting.

To pit plant, dig a hole about one and a half times the width of a garden spade or spit (a long spade with a narrow blade). Gauge the right depth, measuring by eye from the longest root tip to the mark on the tree stem that shows where soil met air while it was planted in the nursery (the collar). Pile the removed soil to one side. If it's a big, expensive sapling, put a little compost in the base and add some mulch if the soil is heavy with clay. Otherwise, it's straight in with the seedling. Push the roots down and make sure they are all well within the hole, holding the stem with one hand while you, or a helper, pile the soil back in. When the soil has filled the hole, gently draw the seedling up to the point where the collar is level with the ground. Then – and this is vital – firm the soil in around the roots with your heel. I usually carry a tub of extra soil in case I need to top up a hole dug into turf or weedy ground. If the tree needs to be protected by a rabbit guard or tube (there are many types, so get advice from your local tree nursery) it goes on now. Carefully hold any twigs or remaining leaves with one hand so that they are not damaged while you slide the tube down the stem. Drive a stake through the ties in the tube and firmly secure it into the ground. Check the stake periodically to make sure it has not come loose.

A second major failure in planting comes when autumn and winter gales rock a new sapling back and forth, introducing air pockets around the roots – which is why staking is so important. But a tree must gain its own strength by bending to the wind, so the modern rule of thumb when planting without a protecting tube is to tie the stake to the tree quite low to the ground to allow the stem to flex naturally. The same method goes for planting trees that have been grown in pots, except that they come with their own compost so you won't need any extra soil. When planting a potted seedling, first water the tree in the pot – generously. Dig a hole in the ground a few inches wider than the pot, to loosen up the surrounding soil and allow the roots to expand naturally. Again, make sure that the collar is level with the ground surface.

A second method, used widely when you are planting 'whips' (one-year-old seedlings with few side branches or just a single stem) by the hundred or thousand, is the notch. It's quicker but not guaranteed to succeed – in other words, expect a few more failures. Insert a spit or spade to the right depth for the roots, kicking down on it with a firm boot to get it well into the ground. Then lever the spade towards you, drop the seedling in, remove the spade and with your boot press the sides of the slit back together. You can add a tube or spiral and stake the tree in the same way as with pit planting. Even with the most assiduous planting, I keep a close eye on trees during their first winter – righting those saplings that the wind has blown over and making sure the soil around the roots is nice and firm. Then in spring comes the pleasure of seeing them burst into leaf.

With pit planting I expect about 95 per cent success; a little less with notch planting. Standing back after a long day's planting and seeing a new woodland in its infancy, with your mind's eye picturing it as a woodland in a few years' time, is an extraordinarily satisfying privilege.

One more tip: don't be tempted to place turf back around the base of a freshly planted tree: the grass will compete with your tree for water and nutrients. Instead, pile some mulch around the base or use a mulch mat (see 'Weeding' in Section 6, page 121).

Trees from a nursery

Whips (see page 92) are easily lifted from the soil, bundled and bagged and, therefore, are cheap to produce and buy. They are ideal for notch planting in bulk because their roots are not yet well developed. Most new plantations are created with whips. In normal woodland creation schemes, which may attract a grant (see Useful information, page 161), whips are planted at a density of about 1500 per hectare (600 per acre). If you imagine a square with 100-metre (330-ft) sides and plant at intervals of 2 metres (6½ ft), you would get 50 trees in a row, and 50 rows, or 2500 to the hectare, but it is recognised that woods need open spaces for glades and rides. So a 2-metre (6½-ft) gap between trees over 60 per cent of the total area of the plot is the standard. Whips can cost as little as 35 pence each when bought in bulk; but one has to add the cost of protection and, if required, chemical weeding. I don't use chemicals in Thistle Wood: instead I mulch with squares of cardboard, or trample unwanted weeds and long grass.

Larger bare-root and potted trees need to be pit planted. They cost more to produce, are bulkier and require a larger investment of time – but they have the advantage of being already more advanced, so they are ideal for those with a generous budget and an inclination to impatience. I find that a mix of whips for bulk and a smaller number of grown-on potted trees is ideal for establishing a diverse age structure right at the start of a woodland project. My best buys are silver birch and rowan trees, already at about 1.2 metres (4 ft) tall, either bare-rooted or in pots. They cost about £2 or £2.50 each, but are well worth it. I might plant a hundred or so in winter, filling in spaces where whips have died or creating a dense area of planting for visual effect. Each plant has a better chance of success than any individual whip. The larger the tree in the nursery, the more it will cost: you can easily pay £50 or £100 for a standard (more than 2 metres or 6½ feet in height) or half-standard tree; well worth it for instant effect if you have the money.

Trees for free

Trees need a means of dispersing their seed so that they don't all fall beneath their parent, where they are less likely to survive. Trees use wind, water, birds and mammals to transport their seeds to an appropriate distance. Some birds swallow fruit and excrete the seeds elsewhere in their territory; some birds and mammals hoard nuts underground and forget where they are. Tree planters rate seeds by what they call 'dormancy': that means that many need special treatment before they will germinate. In the case of berries (fleshy fruits) – from hawthorn, rowan, whitebeam, cherry and so on – a hard seed case is coated with substances that inhibit germination until they have been removed by the action of acids in a bird's stomach. See 'Growing trees from seed', page 99.

Many trees can be propagated for very little cost – it's just a question of budget and patience (or impatience) and the potential satisfaction of growing from seed or from a cutting. Cut a rod off a willow tree in late winter and stick it in the ground and the chances are it'll grow; plant a hundred acorns in autumn and most of them will become oak trees. The following are some simple tips for collecting and sowing seeds, taking cuttings and other methods for growing trees without buying them. It is important to remember two things, though: one is to ask permission if you want to collect seed or take a cutting from a tree on private land. The other is to ensure that you use seed from a tree that is healthy and grows as close to its final planting spot as possible. Planting Scots pine seeds from Norfolk on a Scottish hillside or vice versa is a no-no. Local is best.

Collecting seeds

Autumn is the time for collecting and sowing seeds. Ripe nuts are dull green or brown and can be collected from the ground as they fall, although the first nuts shed by a tree are often not the best specimens. Collect them in a paper or cloth bag and label them if you are not confident about telling them apart. It's worth keeping a seed-collecting diary so that you can look back and see which nuts and seeds from which trees have been the most successful.

Winged seeds can be picked straight from the tree as soon as they are brown. Berries and other fleshy fruits are ripe when they are at their richest colour, sometimes deep into winter. Collect cones from the tree or ground when they have turned brown – late on in autumn. Keep them dry in a paper bag until the seeds have dropped out of the cone. The Tree Council maintains a very useful website that organises, and offers advice on, seed gathering: www.treecouncil.org.uk/Take-Part/Seed-Gathering-Season.

Growing trees from seed –
how to mimic nature

Nuts

The larger, fleshy nuts – acorns, hazelnuts, beech nuts and conkers (although the horse chestnut is not a native) – are the easiest to propagate, because they carry ample reserves of the energy that a new seedling needs to establish itself. Drop the nuts into a bowl or bucket of water and fish out and discard those that float. Bury the good nuts in pots or directly into the ground, about 4 centimetres (1½ in.) below the surface, and let nature do the rest. I reckon on about a 70 per cent success rate: so if you want 70 trees, plant 100 acorns.

Pick the best and freshest nuts and don't leave them around the house in a paper bag to get dry – just go right ahead and plant them as soon as you can after collecting them, two or three to a pot. With beech nuts, many of the shiny brown seed casings do not contain an active kernel, but with practice you'll find you can tell full from empty by gently squeezing them – the fat ones have nuts in. I find myself eating quite a few beech nuts as I sort them – they're delicious. Some tree growers stratify beech and hazel nuts (see the next section); but I've never found it necessary.

Winged seeds

The seeds of field maple and hornbeam don't need to be separated from their 'wings', but they do require stratification – a process by which you can mimic the natural conditions of a winter needed to break the dormancy of the seed – and in some cases two winters. Stratification is simple; you will need: equal volumes of peat-free potting compost; sand, bark chipping or grit; and seeds. Mix everything together well, then put the mix into a well-drained pot, cover and keep in a cool shady spot. Come the spring, you can tip out the mixture and see if any seeds are sprouting green. If they are, carefully take them out and sow them in pots of compost and watch them grow. Put the rest of the mixture back in its pot and have another look in a week or so. Be patient: nature can be capricious.

Fleshy fruits

The fruits of rowan, hawthorn, crab apple and holly also require stratification; but they must first have their flesh removed. Put them in a sieve and rub them under water, or mash them with a potato masher, then rinse, and discard any seeds that float. The seeds from fleshy fruits all need to be stratified to mimic not just the effects of winter but also the conditions inside a bird's stomach.

Cones

The seeds of alder and Scots pine cones should be sown directly into moist compost in pots, two or three at a time. Keep the pots in a cool, shady spot and see what emerges in spring.

Cuttings and layering:
DIY propagation

Fruit trees, hollies and other so-called ornamentals are expensive to buy, but even in a small woodland it is worth having some of these. A cheap alternative to purchase is to learn the arts of taking hardwood cuttings and of grafting.

There is any amount of advice on how to propagate holly trees from cuttings – but some of it is contradictory. My advice would be to try a few methods and see which is the most successful for you; but, basically, the technique is as follows: towards the end of the year select a healthy stem from the current year's growth. Cut it from the tree at right angles with secateurs, then diagonally at the top end so that you have a stem between 20 centimetres (8 in.) and 30 centimetres (12 in.) long, and leave a healthy bud at the top. Dip the bottom end in hormone rooting powder or gel and place two or three into a pot of compost with a layer of sand at the base. Make sure that about two-thirds of the stem, with no leaves, lies below the soil surface. Keep the compost moist and frost-free. The buds should sprout the following spring. Give the cutting a year in its pot before planting out; if two or more shoots come up in a pot, separate them after their first growing season and pot them on individually.

Willows are the easiest trees to propagate. Cut rods off as for holly, then place them in a pot of compost or directly into the ground, firming down the soil around them – there is no need to use a rooting hormone. Make sure they are well-watered in their first year. In spring they will produce shoots – tentatively at first and then vigorously.

I tend to grow these cuttings in small tube shelters attached to a cane for the first year, to keep rabbits and rodents away while they take root. Plant densely, then transplant excess shoots elsewhere.

Grafting: an age-old skill

The grafting of a shoot (scion) of one species of tree onto the rootstock of another seems to have been going on for thousands of years. The armies of Alexander the Great are said to have domesticated the apple by bringing grafts back from the Tien Shan Mountains of Kazakhstan, where it grows wild in abundant variety.

You can buy rootstock from a good local nursery, or you can grow it from the pips of a locally grown crab apple – the best rootstock for the domesticated varieties. Take a healthy cutting with strong buds, in late autumn or in a frost-free part of winter, from the tree you wish to 'copy' and make sure that the lowest part of its stem is of the same diameter as the rootstock that you will graft it to – roughly 6 millimetres (¼ in.) across. Using a very sharp knife, make fresh, upward-slanting cuts and a 'tongue' on both rootstock and scion where they join, bind with a natural twine or floral tape and cover with wax to protect against disease. Pot up the graft and keep cool and moist for a few weeks. There is plenty of more detailed advice in many books and online on the details and techniques of successful grafting (see Further reading, page 167).

One of life's pleasures is the gift of giving, and there's a lot to be said for being able to make a present of trees that you have raised from seed or cutting, for friends and relations or for a local school. I have a small informal nursery at home – my daughter, Flora, tells me that there are fifty-six seedlings in it at present. Many of these will end up in Thistle Wood, while others will find a spot in the garden; but I'll always be able to give a few away at Christmas or for birthdays.

Suitability

Not all trees are suitable for every soil, site and space. Think hard about what a tree will look like when it is mature – will it be too close to a building; will it offer welcome shade or too much dingy shadow; will it potentially mask a view that you don't want to see – or one that you like? Some trees are gregarious (they like to be with others of their own kind), such as beech and Scots pine; others, such as rowans, are perfectly happy as individuals. Some trees are more particular than others about the soils they grow in – heavy or light, clay or sandy, lime or acid, wet or dry. If in doubt about the most suitable trees to plant in your garden or plot, check a reliable tree guide or, perhaps even better, see what trees are doing well in similar conditions nearby.

Tools

I find myself using the same few dependable tools time and again: a long-tongued spade, called a spit, for planting; a very sharp, small hand axe for trimming and to use as a hammer for knocking in stakes; a pair of good, sharp, robust secateurs; and a small pruning saw to remove damaged branches. I usually carry a pocketful of cable ties, too, in case a tree needs re-staking or a tube needs securing. For trimming thin branches and for coppicing youngish trees I use a pair of sturdy long-handled loppers. For most work with established trees I will always carry a billhook, the traditional tool of the woodsman that has never been improved upon. There are many styles, and I like to buy mine second hand. I use both a traditional scythe and a wheeled strimmer to keep the grass down on the rides.

I have used the same chainsaw for more than twenty years; looked after, they'll last for ever.

Mine is one of the smaller but best-quality models – it's less heavy work and less dangerous than a monster with a 20-inch bar. I ALWAYS wear the full safety gear (helmet with visor, ear-defenders, rip-stop trousers, gloves and chainsaw boots) and have been trained to use and maintain the saw safely. I would very strongly advise that anyone using a chainsaw does the same. When you have an accident with a chainsaw, things go wrong fast, and seriously so.

Shelters, fences, guards: pluses, minuses, costs and labour

You might not need to provide much protection for your trees, but the chances are that a whole host of creatures will have designs on them. Rodents eat roots from below; deer, rabbits and hares munch fresh shoots and strip bark; birds nip off juicy buds and many an insect will welcome the chance to lay its eggs on the leaves, or just eat them. Trees are used to this sort of abuse and cope very well on the whole, but if you are planting in an area with deer or rabbits, your trees will need help. Translucent corrugated plastic tubes keep them safe and give them an extra climatic boost in their first years – well worth the cost of about £2 each, plus a stake to keep them solidly upright. There are now many types of tube shelter, so think about which is most suitable; for instance, rabbit spirals will protect hedging plants in their first years.

Buying in bulk is much cheaper than buying these individually. Some shelters claim to be biodegradable; but you'll need to remove them before they rot, because by that time they are probably restricting your tree's ability to breathe through its bark – an essential for good tree health.

6. LOOKING AFTER TREES

Water, warmth, sunlight

Trees are highly adapted, complex and resilient organisms. From a simple premise – convert light to sugar, carry sugar in a water solution, and get bigger every year – trees have evolved sophisticated mechanisms for exploiting the opportunities that nature offers. They rely on just five hormones, which govern growth and their reaction to light; the manufacture of sugars and more complex substances like lignin or tannins; timings for growth and the discarding of leaves in autumn. Like all other plants, trees need sunlight, warmth, water and a small but important group of minerals, occurring in soils, that dissolve in water and can be drawn up through their roots.

Newly planted trees will die if they are heavily browsed by deer or rabbits, if their roots work loose and dry out, or if there is insufficient moisture in the soil for them to develop in their new environment. If you plant a tree, make sure you water it regularly in its first year. When tree leaves droop it is a sure sign of either disease or insufficient water to photosynthesise light successfully in its leaves. You cannot realistically water all the seedlings in a newly planted woodland, so you have to accept a certain proportion of failures and for that reason initial planting density is deliberately generous. Planting in autumn gives woodland trees their best chance of becoming established at the least stressful time of year, with the most ample soil moisture. In springtime, tree growth is triggered by daylight length and rising soil temperatures: most plants won't grow until the soil has been warmed above 6°C or so for a couple of weeks.

Disease and failure

Trees attract parasites, fungi and other diseases, many of which are just unsightly, but some may also be deadly. Oak leaves become mildewy in middle to late summer; they attract gall wasps that lay eggs on their leaves; and the leaves are eaten by caterpillars. Somehow the tree survives and, in shedding leaves and growing a fresh set annually, they remain vigorous for hundreds of years. Some diseases are much more serious: ash dieback (*Chalara fraxinea*), which was brought into the UK with diseased imports from Europe some years ago, threatens to devastate our ash trees. Dutch elm disease has emptied the British landscape of all but a few mature elms (they still thrive in hedgerows and woods, but only up to a certain age, after which they succumb to the bark beetle that carries the disease). Arboriculturists warn of even nastier potential imports, from America and elsewhere, that may threaten even our resilient oaks. If you are concerned about the appearance of a tree in your wood or garden, get expert advice from a local nursery or tree surgeon or go online for support. The Forestry Commission maintains a website with helpful identification tips and advice on safe disposal and treatments (see Section 4, page 51).

Sometimes, for no apparent reason, a tree will give up the ghost. Often that is because of something going on underground: moles munching on roots, for example. A couple of years ago I was given a splendid half-standard rowan tree by some friends and I planted it in a very prominent place in Thistle Wood. All looked fine until late May, when the leaves dried, shrivelled and fell off. To all intents and purposes the tree had just died for no apparent reason. Knowing a little about tree biology, I wondered if I might fool the tree into reviving itself, so I snipped the ends off all of its branches and twigs with a pair of secateurs. My idea was to 'switch off' the hormone auxin, which is most concentrated in the growing tips of trees. Auxin promotes growth in the tips but suppresses the emergence of lateral buds all the way along the stem, where they lie dormant beneath the bark. When the tip of a tree is damaged in a storm, or by browsing, side shoots emerge to compensate: the tree bushes out, then recovers and heads for the sky once more. A few days after this last-ditch experiment, I noticed small green buds swelling on the stem of my rowan. Two weeks later it was in leaf again, then at last, very late in the season, it flowered and produced tiny berries. My advice is that, unless you have a very obvious disease that requires treating or disposal, give a tree a chance to recover on its own, or coppice it close to the ground. I will allow a tree twelve months to revive before I give up on it.

Pruning

Gardeners like to trim trees to improve fruit yields and to enhance their natural form. In a small garden, or when growing trees in containers, pruning is a necessity. Most trees respond well to pruning, so long as you don't cut the side branches too closely to the main stem. Leave the 'collar' (visible where the branch or twig is joined to the main stem) intact to help prevent disease. If in doubt, consult your local nursery or a good gardening book. Otherwise, it's a matter of taste. I prune damaged branches and stems to help prevent disease and, for a crop of trees that will produce timber, I side-prune to give a straight, knot-free trunk. Where trees have been badly damaged by browsing animals I will normally coppice them (see below) to give them the best chance of a fresh start.

Coppicing

Trees have been browsed, attacked and generally abused by other creatures for millions of years and have evolved to respond by sending out new shoots, 'switching off' the hormone auxin (see above). Humans have learned to take advantage of this natural phenomenon by coppicing: cutting a tree down close to the ground so that it sends up multiple new shoots. These shoots tend to grow very straight and, when cut every few years, enable the woodsman or -woman to produce a crop of poles for a variety of uses, including construction.

Traditional British coppice species included the ubiquitous hazelnut, ash, oak, hornbeam, small-leaved lime, elm, beech, alder and the non-native sweet chestnut. As a rural craft, coppicing very nearly died out in the late twentieth century; it is now being revived as a wholly sustainable, locally focused industry producing hurdles, charcoal, fencing materials and lightweight timber. Trees continually managed by coppicing live longer than those allowed an ordinary life cycle: a small miracle of the partnership between humans and nature.

Most trees respond positively to coppicing; some, such as the silver birch, are less enthusiastic as they get older and may not survive. Coppicing can be carried out all year round, but is best left to autumn and winter when the tree is dormant. If you coppice between August and October you risk fresh buds being caught by the first frosts before they have had a chance to harden off. The cycle of coppicing a parcel of woodland every few years produces a unique habitat cycle of light and shade, which has been shown to be the most biologically rich and diverse environment in our temperate maritime climate. Flowers, grasses and lichens perfectly adapted to coppiced woodlands form a unique and very special community and, as such, they are often used as indicators of the presence of ancient woodland.

Pollarding

Where trees and animals mix, the trees eventually lose out to grazing. A form of land management known as wood pasture, which was for hundreds of years a common sight in our countryside, involved pollarding – cutting trees at a stem height out of the reach of sheep and cattle and getting the best of both worlds. Willow pollards are still a common sight in fenlands and along river banks and you can spot the signs of former pollarding management on trees whose trunks branch out from about head-height upwards. The stupendous hornbeam groves of Epping Forest in south-west Essex show just such traces of former management.

Weeding

All professional arboriculturists and foresters recommend weeding around young trees, because grasses and other plants compete for moisture and minerals in the soil. In scientific tests, this is borne out by the evidence. Cutting grass around trees only encourages it to grow, so it's best not to. Some planters, like me, don't much like using chemical herbicides, so I either mulch with bark or make individual mulch mats for trees using waste cardboard; alternatively, I trample – kicking down any grasses or thistles around a newly planted tree for its first two or three years. A mat of rotting or dead vegetation around the base of a tree is certainly better than bare soil.

Trees are pretty ruthless when it comes to competition: eventually they shade out annuals and perennials, send their roots deeper and further than any herbaceous plants, and create the dense canopy that wins the day.

7. WATCHING TREES

know a few of the trees in Thistle Wood really well – they have become my acquaintances and I make sure to pass the time of day with them on a regular basis. They are my bellwethers, telling me the state of the season and marking the stages in their growth from planting. If I coppice or prune them I go back to check how they are doing. I'm fascinated when an oak develops wasp or spangle galls; when its leaves go mildewy in late summer. I like to watch as the rowans flower and the flowers turn into yellow then red berries, picked off one after another by the birds.

Now that camera traps are easily available and coming down in price, I have one attached to a pole at the edge of the new pond: here I can vicariously catch sight of deer and foxes and of the many birds that visit the pond to drink and bathe and generally socialise with each other. These camera traps often also have time-lapse functions: you can set one up to watch a particular tree for a whole year and make a film of its progress – and it's surprising how much more detail and knowledge you acquire when you can see an entire year pass by in just a few minutes of video. But it's also good just to walk into a wood, sit beneath the spreading boughs of a tree, and watch the world go by: the more you watch, the more you will notice.

The four seasons: what trees get up to and when

Autumn

This is the start of the woodland year. Just when you might think that trees are settling down for the winter, they are in fact busy storing, recycling and preparing. Most trees' buds for the following year, and even their catkins, have already developed by now and are hardening off before the first frosts. Precious sugars and minerals are being recycled from leaves into a tree's storage reserves, producing, as a by-product, all those wonderful reds, oranges, yellows, purples and browns that enrich the autumn countryside or garden. Fruits and nuts are falling or have fallen, been borne off by the wind or squirrelled away by acquisitive animals and birds. In the process, the seeds of new tree crops have been sown by forgetful jays (acorns) and small mammals (hazelnuts, beech nuts, etc.), ready to send up their first shoots when spring arrives. Birds are busy eating berries from hawthorns, hollies, rowans, cherries and black-thorn and when these pass through their guts they are ready to be cooled by winter's frosts – all part of the essential processes that will ready the seeds for germination.

Winter

At this time of year trees are not totally inactive, whatever their external appearance might suggest. They must protect against frost and – paradoxically – the drought conditions that prolonged frost can bring. Some trees, such as the holly, manufacture oils that effectively work like anti-freeze. Others, such as birches and maples, wait until spring to show off their survival tricks. Trees must be strong enough to withstand high winds, too. Many trees will shed smaller, outer twigs and branches on windy days, while the effect of steady prevailing winds is to strengthen the tree. Conifers and broad-leaved trees add muscle to limbs and trunks differently: generally speaking, conifers push against pressure, and broad-leaved trees pull towards it, compensating for slopes, winds, the loss of branches and partial wind-throw.

Winter weather and shorter days induce dormancy in British trees – all their internal chemical processes slow down and, at temperatures below about 6°C, the roots stop drawing up water and nutrients altogether. Trees are no longer producing food but storing it in their vessels and the rays that connect them. To protect buds from triggering their new growth during short periods of mild winter weather, dormancy is set, like the alarm on a safe, not to end too quickly. For the tree enthusiast, it is a great season to appreciate the structure of a tree and its distinctness from other species. Conifers remain in leaf, their tall conical shapes ideal for collecting energy from the low sun. The domed shapes of more temperate trees now show themselves – adapted for the arc of the summer sun in the higher latitudes. It's now quite easy to identify many trees from the way the buds form: beech buds are like sharp pen nibs or the ends of knitting needles; oak buds form fist-like clusters; those of the ash tree are, uniquely, jet black.

Spring

Now trees are busy. As soon as the soil temperature climbs above 6°C for more than a fortnight
or so, growth processes are triggered. As daylight
hours increase, buds will burst. The first leaves
to emerge in a wood are those of the climbing
honeysuckle, taking advantage before they are
shaded out. Cherries are quick to respond to
warmer, longer days. Rowans will sprout in early
April; birch, willow and hazel follow, while the
first rich green fuzz of the hedgerows offers the
promise of blossom to come. Oak, beech and ash
are the slowest of our native trees to come into
leaf, often as late as the end of May. Some leaves
are preceded by catkins and blossom.

Spring is not without its problems for some
trees. Prolonged hard frosts can cause air cavi-
ties in the vertically stacked vessels of many
tree species as the ice melts, breaking the water
column and potentially killing the tree. Maples
and birches, in particular, have adapted by being

able to generate positive water pressure in their roots, forcing out air pockets higher up the tree and, like an old diesel engine, repriming the water column. I like to keep a record of when the trees in Thistle Wood sprout their leaves and blossoms. After a very mild winter in 2016–17, trees were pretty quick to respond to the longer days; but in the winter of 2017–18 all was delayed by about three weeks because of the prolonged cold and wet: it seemed as if spring would never arrive. But trees are patient creatures: they bide their time and during the summer they catch up.

Summer

Following that miserable winter, we suddenly found ourselves in near-drought conditions – much more serious for trees, especially those planted in the previous autumn that haven't had time to establish their roots. I am watching the 100 birches and 40 rowans that I planted very carefully and, as each week goes by with temperatures in the high 20°C and no sign of rain, one after another is wilting, their leaves turning brown. In the garden and when growing container trees, it is vital that you help them with water. On the larger scale of the plantation, one can only watch and hope for rain. But the oaks and cherries are thriving, putting on about an inch of height every week. The bigger, more mature trees can easily cope with a dry summer, especially after so much rain in the late part of winter and early spring. Beech trees are much more prone to suffer from drought, so any young beech hedges should be watered – unless you have a local ban on hosepipes.

It's also interesting, at this time of the year, to watch the insects and spiders, butterflies and birds doing their reproductive thing. At my new pond, I have been watching videos from the camera trap of magpie parents showing their young how to take a proper bath: admirable parenting exemplars.

What leaves tell us

Quite apart from their vital function in absorbing the sun's energy and converting it into sugars, leaves tell us a great deal about the trees on which they grow. Each species has optimised its adaptation to a particular niche and the leaves give clues to those niches. Pine needles are thin, dark and covered in a waxy coating: since they stay on the tree for the whole year, they can utilise even the weak sun of winter – hence the dark green colour, very efficient at absorbing low levels of light. The wax helps them to prevent water loss in dry conditions and their thinness helps the tree to shed snow in winter. The trembling leaf of the aspen (*Populus tremula*) allows it to evaporate water very efficiently even in the gentlest breeze, so the tree can drink huge quantities of water, enabling it to exploit low concentrations of minerals. This is an adaptation to both high rainfall and poor soils (like those on Scotland's west coast).

Leaves with pointed tips shed rainwater fast; large leaves enable some of the so-called canopy trees – such as oak and sycamore – to shade out the competition.

There is also a difference between leaves that spend their lives in full sunlight and those, called shade leaves, that don't get so much sun: the latter are more efficient than their full-sun counterparts. By the end of summer, leaves are looking tired; their shining spring green colour has dulled; they are probably pock-marked with insect chewing, or with infestations such as spangle galls or black spots. In hot, dry weather leaves will hang limp: they simply cannot take up enough water to process the energy they are gaining from the sun, and they shut down or go slow. In autumn, deciduous trees are recycling precious sugars and minerals for winter storage and preparing to shed their leaves in a complex process called abscission. But even then, their replacements for next year will already be in place, primed to respond to the warmer soils and longer daylight hours of spring.

Tree behaviour and character

Trees don't think, plan, calculate or strategise, and yet their range of behaviours is so complex and focused that it's tempting to credit them with all the arts and devices of humans or animals. Some trees aggressively suppress others by out-competing them for light or by exhaling poisons. Trees respond to external threats – wind-throw, drought, ice or animal attack – with a bewildering armoury of countermeasures that includes the prickly leaves of holly, the tannin poison in oak, the ability to regrow after cutting and to send up new stems towards the light when blown over. Veteran trees, such as stag-headed oaks or vast hollow yews, seem almost to take on the characters of elderly sages, indomitable forces for stability and repositories of wisdom and history.

Because they cannot move and bring themselves into direct physical contact with potential sexual partners, they have evolved instead to send their pollen, or have it couriered, to their mates, sufficient to ensure seed production.

Over thousands of years humans have studied tree behaviour and learned to imitate it for their own ends, as well as exploiting trees for their bounty of fuel, materials, medicines, shelter and food. We can increase the reliability of pollination and seed production, trigger tree hormones, propagate by cutting and grafting and prune trees to create more or less any shape we fancy. Trees seem to be assiduous students of nature and they have been adapting to the slings and arrows of evolution for over 300 million years, so they are well-qualified teachers. We humans are their prize pupils.

Trees and other trees:
loners and crowds

Some trees do very well on their own. In the tropical rainforests many grow far away from their nearest relatives, while in temperate woodlands you often find large numbers of only two or three dominant species. Some trees, such as the oaks, are so dominant that they create what is called climax vegetation, engineering a continuous canopy over the land and shading out all competition. Like the other so-called gregarious species, oaks grow with others of their own kind for sound biological reasons: cooperation and the suppression of competition. Scots pines and beeches are also gregarious, sharing an intimate and beneficial relationship with underground fungi and forming a highly complex ecosystem of their own. Trees that produce berries and fleshy fruits tend to be loners – their seed-distribution partners ensuring that the next generation doesn't grow too close to the parent.

One fascinating aspect of forest trees is how, from a distance, the profile of hundreds of trees against the horizon looks like a single organism, each growing to the same height, with those at the edge sloping down towards the ground and any little gap in the canopy filled so that the whole woodland has a smooth profile.

Wildlife and trees; woodland flowers to enhance your trees

Trees in woodlands are keystones of a very complex and rich habitat. Many creatures, fungi and lichens live directly on or in trees, or feed off them. The soils of a woodland are rich in nutrients, while the shade from the trees keeps down aggressive, light-hungry plants like the grasses. Woodlands are stable, air-conditioned environments, lessening extremes of temperature and providing a stable habitat for a whole suite of other plants. Many flowers respond well to the woodland environment, and upwards of forty species are regarded as indicators that a woodland is ancient. Bluebells are perhaps the best known, but there are other woody marvels, too: wood anemone and wood sorrel (whose clover-like leaves are edible), wild garlic (also edible), moschatel, oxlip and many more. Some of these spring-flowering species are adapted to the cycles of light and shade provided by periodic coppicing. Plant some of these in your garden woodland glade and their flowers and foliage will add to the richness of the environment that you have created.

Only ever buy wild-flower seeds or plants from reputable sources. It is illegal to collect whole plants from the wild but you can collect a few ripe seeds for personal use from plants that are not endangered.

8. FAMOUS TREE PLANTERS

John Evelyn (1620–1706)

Few books on forestry have had greater impact than John Evelyn's *Sylva, or A Discourse on Forest Trees and the Propagation of Timber in His Majesty's Dominions,* published in 1664 during the reign of Charles II. It ran to five editions in his lifetime. It is both an encyclopaedic account of native and non-native trees and their management and a call for the planting of new woodlands; it is also remarkable for Evelyn's understanding of the importance of soil in tree health. It followed an important earlier work of 1615 by Arthur Standish – a pamphlet of just thirty-four pages – called *New Directions of Experience... for the Increasing of Timber and Firewood.*

Admiral Collingwood (1748–1810)

Cuthbert Collingwood spent most of his life at sea in the Royal Navy. He rose through the ranks to become Nelson's second-in-command at the Battle of Trafalgar in 1805. He was celebrated for his humanity and for his care of ordinary seamen, while his letters home are full of a wistful longing for his beloved Northumberland.

He knew a great deal about wood: his career was spent, as he put it himself, with no more than a six-inch oak plank between himself and eternity. He knew the properties of wood and of people and made much of their similarities. He valued his native landscape as only an exile can. From a lonely posting in the Western Mediterranean during his last years he commissioned the planting of an oak woodland on an estate that he inherited and the Collingwood oaks still grow on the slopes of a hill in the College Valley on the Anglo-Scottish border. The Admiral encouraged his fellow countrymen to plant acorns in hedgerows so that Britain's navy should never lack the timber she needed to build ships – her wooden walls.

John Chapman (1774–1845)

Better known to history as Johnny Appleseed, Chapman was a nurseryman and an eccentric, itinerant preacher of the American Midwest. He was apprenticed to an orchardist in Ohio, but the first of his many nurseries for growing apple trees was planted in Warren, Pennsylvania. Many legends grew up telling of his kindness and quirkiness; but the facts of his achievement in developing America's precious fruit orchards are undeniable: at his death he left an estate of 490 hectares (1200 acres) of nurseries.

Jean Giono (1895–1970)

The French writer Jean Giono created the allegorical character of a Provençal shepherd, Elzéard Bouffier, for a short story called, in English, *The Man Who Planted Trees*. Day after day, year after year, Bouffier planted acorns and beech nuts on the desolate, arid, depopulated slopes of the northern Pyrenees, unwitnessed by a world busy with war and wealth. After four decades the valleys and hills once more became green and the people returned, believing that the reforestation of the region was a natural, almost miraculous event. Giono's storytelling was so unaffected and convincing that many readers believed it to be true, and the story of Elzéard Bouffier has inspired many real-life tree planters.

Wangari Maathai (1940–2011) and the Green Belt Movement

A Kenyan academic and political activist in a country ruled by an authoritarian government, Professor Wangari Maathai made the association between environmental degradation, food poverty and the disempowerment and oppression of the rural poor and realised that the solution must be internal and 'grass roots'. She founded the Green Belt Movement in 1977 to empower women and their local communities to create sustainable, productive land where before it was barren. She trained 30,000 women and between them they planted 35 million trees.

Maathai believed that in tree planting there is 'agency': it is not just an activity but a statement and a signature of authorship in a landscape. Arrested, assaulted and imprisoned on several occasions, she was eventually elected to the Kenyan parliament, achieved worldwide recognition and was made a Nobel Peace Prize Laureate in 2004. Her book, *The Green Belt Movement*, was published in 2003. She is regarded as the inspiration for the global Billion Tree Campaign: www.plant-for-the-planet.org/en/treecounter/billion-tree-campaign-2.

The race to reforestation

Across the world initiatives are planned or underway to plant trees on an epic scale. The Great Green Wall is a hugely ambitious African Union scheme, involving eleven countries, to create a mosaic of green, productive landscapes right across the southern edge of advancing desert regions in North Africa, the Sahel and as far east as the Horn of Africa – over 4,000 miles. Local farming initiatives in Niger and Burkina Faso have shown how careful management of water resources and existing trees, and knowledge of native plants, may hold the key to a greener future. A similar plan in

Asia, the Green Great Wall of China, aims to hold back the Gobi Desert and provide sustainable land for the future.

Following the pioneering work of the Indian civil servant S. M. Raju, Indian volunteers created a new record in 2017 when they planted 66 million trees in just twelve hours in the state of Madhya Pradesh, outdoing their neighbours in Uttar Pradesh who, in 2016, had planted 50 million trees in a day.

In the UK, The National Forest was established at the end of the last century to enrich part of the English Midlands where only 6 per cent of land lay under woodland cover. Since then, more than 8 million trees have been planted, covering 200 square miles, stimulating the recovery of woodland habitats, bringing visitors to the area and fostering businesses dependent on woodland produce: www.nationalforest.org. Have a look at a satellite image of the Midlands and see if you can see The National Forest from space.

The Queen's Commonwealth Canopy is a network of forestry conservation and planting projects across the fifty-three countries of the Commonwealth, established with the aim not just of conserving forests and their habitats but also of providing an educational resource and knowledge exchange forum to support future international collaboration.

If you belong to a school interested in planting and understanding trees, why not set up a partnership with other schools across the Commonwealth to share ideas and interests in conservation and diversity?

9. WHAT SHALL WE DO WITH ALL THE TREES?

Leave them alone

Periodically, government agencies encourage tree-planting schemes of more or less ambitious proportions. Britain, after all, is one of the least-wooded countries in Europe, a function of both its size and the land's suitability for agriculture. One hears less often about what to do with all those trees after they have been planted. There is something to be said for letting nature get on with it, leaving the trees we plant to fend for themselves, creating assets for future generations to decide what to do with them. We might also allow formerly managed and ancient woods to follow their own fortunes. There are compelling reasons for doing so: we interfere so much with nature that there ought to be room for places where we just leave it alone. And in any case, the more trees there are stabilising landscapes, absorbing carbon dioxide and pollutants and breathing out oxygen for us, the better.

The other side of the debate stresses the value of the human/nature relationship: the richness of traditionally managed woodland, the value of rural employment and of utilising our own resources instead of importing most of our timber and charcoal at the expense of vulnerable environments across the world. One thing is certain, the more publicly the issue is debated, the more likely it is that society can make reasoned, informed choices about habitats that will increasingly matter to following generations.

'Conserve' them?

Tree conservation has become an established movement in the UK, protecting ancient woods from destruction and enhancing a communal sense of caring for the environment. Tree Preservation Orders (TPOs) protect individual specimens of great age or landscape value. Conservation orders protect both the built and natural environment from wanton destruction, but the idea of 'conserving' an ancient woodland is not quite as simple as it seems. Fencing off a long-established wood and leaving the trees alone is a tacit encouragement to a few species to dominate at the expense of other native trees and flowers. A wood that has been managed for centuries and is then left to be 'conserved' loses biodiversity and habitat range, year on year. And where do we draw the line with the species that are to be retained: is a beech tree in the north of England non-native and therefore to be expunged from a wood where beeches have grown for half a millennium? These are not easy questions to resolve.

Plant them in huge numbers?

Britain is the net third-largest importer of wood in the world. Suppose that the British Isles was brought up to the European average of tree cover – about 38 per cent of the land mass, according to recent EU statistics. Currently, according to the Forestry Commission, England has about 10 per cent, Wales 15 per cent, Scotland 18 per cent and Northern Ireland 8 per cent. That covers all woodland and forestry, including large swathes of land planted with non-native conifers, which offer very limited habitat value. If we want to bring the UK up to average, two questions are obvious: what land, habitats and plants would we be replacing (moorland, farmland, reclaimed brownfield sites)?; and which trees should be planted – more non-native, fast-growing conifers to reduce dependence on imported timber; native broadleaves for habitat, flood control and general wellbeing; or a balanced mix of both? The UK's largest new woodland project, on Doddington North Moor in Northumberland, is being planned to address such dilemmas: are they getting it right? (www.doddingtonnorthforest.com/home).

Rewild the land?

In recent years there has been a small movement towards 'rewilding'. In essence, this means fencing off land, usually in hilly areas and wilderness, to protect naturally regenerating vegetation from grazing animals like deer, rabbits and sheep, and then letting nature do its thing. In some cases the idea has been linked with the reintroduction of formerly native animal species, most notably beaver and wolves. Such schemes have triggered debates about what is wild and what is managed landscape, and just how much room there is in a seemingly crowded island for animals that might compete with livestock and other human activities, such as tourism.

Whatever the outcome of the debate, trees will form the pivotal habitat in all rewilding schemes. There are no genuinely wild habitats left in the UK now. Even the apparent remnants of the once great Caledonian forest have been subject to human pressures for thousands of years. But recent schemes in the North-west Highlands of Scotland have shown that rewilding the lower slopes of some of the glens (whose moorland landscapes are, in any case, artificial and driven by animal grazing and game bird management) fosters the reintroduction of many native tree species and the fauna that they host. The results are spectacular and marvellous to see.

Trees for produce

It has often been said that the best protection for trees comes from their economic value, whether that is measured by a tourist economy, timber tonnage, local jobs or savings on flood mitigation and climate change. Trees are perhaps the most sustainable resource that Earth has to offer, bringing multiple benefits not just to nature but to rural and urban communities, too. Those who embrace the pleasures, challenges and satisfaction of planting and growing trees and then creating new arts, crafts and produce from them are their most persuasive champions.

For those who can't plant trees, it's possible to contribute by both supporting those who do, and by trying to buy woodland produce – barbecue charcoal (the UK imports 60,000 tonnes of it a year), timber, firewood, furniture and fencing – from sustainable UK sources and by encouraging local retailers to source their material appropriately. It's also well worth thinking about which plastic products you use and whether there is a natural wood alternative: from log baskets and trugs to clothes horses, tool handles, window frames, breadboards, spoons and garden furniture. The more woodland produce we buy and use, the more incentive there is for the commercial planting and managing of trees, which in turn protects new and established woodlands and rural jobs.

USEFUL INFORMATION

I have a page on my website dedicated to Thistle Wood and I try to post regular updates: www. theambulist.co.uk/sample-page/thistle-wood

Tom Heap's film for the BBC's *Costing the Earth* programme: www.bbc.co.uk/programmes/ bo8r1v9h is a fascinating discussion on the future of woods and forests in the UK.

The most substantial owners and managers of woodlands in the UK are the Forestry Commission, the National Trust and the National Trust for Scotland, the Woodland Trust and the many Wildlife Trusts. Their various websites, listed below, are invaluable sources of information, advice, places to visit and opportunities to volunteer. These are also listed on the Thistle Wood web page, so that you can click and link directly to them.

- www.forestry.gov.uk
- www.nationaltrust.org.uk/trees-and-plants
- www.nationaltrust.org.uk/news/a-new-tree-charter-for-the-21st-century
- www.nts.org.uk/what-we-do/countryside-and-wildlife/key-habitats/woodlands
- www.woodlandtrust.org.uk
- www.woodlandtrust.org.uk/about-us/where-we-work/scotland
- www.woodlandtrust.org.uk/plant-trees/free-trees
- www.woodlandtrust.org.uk/visiting-woods/trees-woods-and-wildlife/british-trees/native-trees
- www.wildlifetrusts.org/closer-to-nature/volunteer

Other volunteering opportunities can be found by contacting The Conservation Volunteers (TCV): www.tcv.org.uk.

For information and advice about setting up a community woodland scheme there is a network: www.communitywoodland.org, while advice on the available grants for woodland creation can be found at: www.forestry.gov.uk/england-woodlandcreation.

There is a network of small woodland owners, too: http://smallwoods.org.uk.

Some notable tree nurseries and suppliers of hedging plants can be found through the following links:

- www.hedgesdirect.co.uk
- www.treesplease.co.uk
- www.trees-online.co.uk
- www.treesdirect.co.uk

There are many more to be found if you search the internet – and local is generally best.

If you want to ensure that your barbecue charcoal is sourced locally from sustainable woodland, there are many reputable suppliers: ncfed.org.uk/public/charcoal-suppliers.

Information on the National Forest can be found here: www.nationalforest.org.

If you are interested in getting involved with the Forest Schools movement, this website has more information: www.forestschoolassociation.org.

The Tree Council has several web pages worth consulting for planting advice, seed gathering events and much more:

- www.treecouncil.org.uk/Take-Part/Seed-Gathering-Season
- www.treecouncil.org.uk/Shop-Donate/Publications
- www.treecouncil.org.uk/About-Us/What-We-Do

For advice on grafting fruit trees, try: www.theorchardproject.org.uk/guides_and_advice/how-to-graft-fruit-trees.

The Sylva Foundation campaigns to bring people and trees closer together: www.sylva.org.uk.

For advice and ideas on building and maintaining a wildlife pond: https://freshwaterhabitats.org.uk/pond-clinic/create-pond/

FURTHER READING

The Collins Complete Guide to British Trees by Paul Sterry (Collins, 2008)

Woodlands: A Practical Handbook by Elizabeth Agate (editor) (British Trust for Conservation Volunteers, 2002)

Flora Britannica by Richard Mabey (Chatto and Windus, 1996)

Wildwood: A Journey Through Trees by Roger Deakin (Penguin, 2008)

Trees and Woods in the British Landscape by Oliver Rackham (Weidenfeld and Nicholson, 2001)

The Hidden Life of Trees by Peter Wohlleben (William Collins, 2017)

The Man Who Planted Trees by Jean Giono (Peter Owen, 1989)

The New Sylva: A Discourse of Forest and Orchard Trees for the Twenty-First Century by Gabriel Hemery and Sarah Simblet (Bloomsbury, 2014)

Forest Gardening by Robert A. de J. Hart (Green Earth Books, 1996)

The Wisdom of Trees by Max Adams (Head of Zeus, 2018)

The Hedge Tree Handbook by Jon Stokes and Kevin Hand (The Tree Council, 2004)

Making Wildlife Ponds: How to Create a Pond to Attract Wildlife to Your Garden (Gardening with Nature Series) by Jenny Steel (Brambleby Books, 2016)

The Green Belt Movement: Sharing the Approach and the Experience by Wangari Maathai (Lantern Books, 2004)